A Visitor Kills Me

Fragments of a Surreal Memoir

Steve Owen

ISBN: 978-81-19654-38-3

First Edition: 2023
Rs. 200/-

Cyberwit.net
HIG 45 Kaushambi Kunj, Kalindipuram
Allahabad - 211011 (U.P.) India
http://www.cyberwit.net
Tel: +(91) 9415091004
E-mail: info@cyberwit.net

Printed at Repro India Limited.

Acknowledgements

A Visitor Kills Me would not be possible without Melanie Rae Thon, who showed me how to phase into people's heads and steal their hidden jelly, and Julia Moncur, who created the cover art for this collection by scraping some jam from between her toes.

Contents

Sunburn

Straight home after school, the Sheriff, who reminded me of a general, said. Stay inside until your parents come home. Don't accept candy (he described the child abductor: a man with a beard who looked like local TV personality Shotgun Tom Kelly). Don't accept rides to Disneyland. Don't engage in conversation. DON'T.

My school, Alpine Elementary, had called us for an assembly. I was in the third grade. Be on alert for a van that looks like the sun, he said. My eyes ached when he said it and I closed them, imagined walking through the door of a brilliantly bright, radioactive sun, with wheels.

As the Sheriff spoke, his hand tapped the black holster on his belt. For emphasis on words like DISNEY and CANDY. My eyes seemed stuck, captured by some invisible force in the GUN, on its black barrel, its door. The hallway. I walked inside, my fingers touching its shiny walls, and lay down beside the bullets, my brothers, in the gun's cylinder. It's cold in here, we thought, are you afraid of being taken? Depends where we go, the bullets said. We don't get out much. We have short cold lives that get caught in strangers' bodies. Then we're trapped alone. Like when L— moved away. What would happen, I asked, if the sun were to steal me, a bullet? I could kill it! I knocked on my steel casing to prove my point. Kill the sun? they mocked. We can't do that. That's what we do! I objected. We're killers! Yes, one said, but the sun is too big and too hot. We'd be deadly as ice. And regardless, another said, you're not a bullet (a third laughed). You're not like us at all! What am I if not a bullet? I thought about knocking myself again, but I was afraid my casing might not make the same sound; my body suddenly seemed more flimsy and weak (my brothers' lack of acceptance was bothering me). Instead I said, How else could I lie down in here? We're the same! What's inside our bellies is much different, they said, you don't know because you're a little slow. Put your hand in and see. I placed my hand on my closest brother's casing and a small grate, a door, appeared, which I opened. Flames licked the interior and stuck out like a tongue and grabbed my hand. Blisters began to bloat my hand, making it look more like a doctor's glove, the kind I'd seen on TV and always thought of blowing up like a balloon. Now my hand was inflated and hurt, so I yanked it away from the tongue. It deflated and returned to the size of my own small hand, and my brothers said, See? Now look past your casing. Before I could pull my shirt up, the Sheriff finished speaking. He turned to shake hands with Mr. Kirby, our principal, and my soul shot from the cylinder, fired from my brothers, back into my own body.

I got off the bus that afternoon and pistoled it home to nab my bike, ready to be abducted. It was a bright spring day. After some time spying unsuccessfully for a sight of the sun, I decided to park on my bike in the middle of the street. This was easy to do because only a few cars came up our road, black-topped Roble Grande, Lookie-Loos usually, because we were in the country and far flung from the center of town. The light banging off the asphalt hurt my eyes, the heat releasing an oily smell which came from the belly of the street. Between myself and my house stood a field of foxtails and a cactus tree. I spent so many hours beneath it, curled up in its shady rocks, staring up at its prickly, expressionless pancake faces, that it was easy to imagine myself there — even with the flaking fence between us — running a finger across a pad, placing my eye before a single spine tip, until I was running along the spine, towards my own areola. We — my cactus family and I — produced a fruit called tuna, which looked like eggs of blood to my human family — specifically, human me — who left them to rot in the sun out of fear, and each summer, migrant farm workers, who my father faithfully called "wetbacks," would ask my mother's permission to pick some, to grill or make into wine, because they were familiar with our delicious bubblegum flavor.

Our faces caught sun from the air, amused at the useless cries of the foxtails rallying around us, attempting to overrun our field with their inferior "spikelets." Stuffing myself as I yawned and stretched my roots further into the ground, I wanted to ask my faceless mother why she wouldn't let me go to L—'s goodbye party, but since our waxy skin and spiny faces made speech too painful, we remained silent, unable to communicate our true intentions, and only the wind moved us at times. I was left with the explanation my human mother had provided: You can catch an infection from a community swimming pool. But not if I'm a cactus, I wanted to say, suspecting, as usual, some hidden reason behind her decision. We eat the sun! We have held this field from invaders, including grazing horses, for generations! L— and I married during Kindergarten: we sat next to each other each day in class, tracing the correct form of letters together, observing the immature behavior of the others (those who missed their parents and lost control of their tempers; those who marched through the block home L— and I created, reducing it to rubble). We remained monogamous the whole year, the intimacy growing between us until we developed a form of telepathy, a shared secret language made up of eye and finger signs, how dare you keep us apart! If she could speak, I believe, then and now, she would have revealed her prejudice against L—'s family, who lived in an apartment complex with a dirty swimming pool — although how she could know this I never knew since she had never been there; or perhaps more likely, it was simply too far to transport me to due to her fear of driving (or both or neither).

I could tell by the slow speed of the orange van rising up the road that my abductor had arrived. The people who lived in our neighborhood often sped down this road, ignoring children, snakes, rabbits, careening home to their own safe, secret lives. Parked on my bike, but also in my cactus body, my mind was caught in both places at once. I saw my splayed shoes on the black top, I saw my mother staring at me, her face a frozen ping pong paddle. My child body felt surprised and wondered if we could become a bullet again. My cactus body was more interested in my mother's sublime reasoning. You will catch a disease! she said. You will drown from lack of supervision! Our swimming pool is dirty for weeks, you let me swim when it's bright yellow, why can't I visit my wife?

The still sun. Stopped in front of me. In my split state, I waited for him to open his door and take me. Instead, my abductor's window rolled down. He had a brown beard, which didn't seem spiky but combed, a soft cushion. He asked me what I was doing, and unable to explain myself, I said, I wanted to talk with him.

His eyelid twitched and my soul returned. Stammering at first, he invited me to sit beside him in the passenger's seat. I placed my bike on the side of the road and opened his door.

As we sat there with the engine running, his hand kept rising to rub his twitching eyelid.

Sweat beaded his forehead, and the walls of the van felt hot and slick. I sensed his suffering, and I reached up to touch his face. His beard was soft, like the cushion I'd imagined, but below the surface, the hair grew thicker, coarse, the skin gone scabby, seedy in patches. Just then, his eyelid twitched. It made me think of a locked door, one banged on repeatedly by something trapped inside. My hand turned into a key and rose up to meet it.

As I touched his eyelid, I caught a glimpse of myself reaching out. My face looked sunburned, my nose snotted with orange mucus. He slapped my hand away and tried to grab my wrist.

I opened the door and leaped. Slammed hard, picked up my bike and started pedaling. My hand stung. I wanted him to chase me. Instead, the van's wheels peeled off and I could feel gassy tar forming in the blacktop's gut, my body, light as it was, sinking into it.

Abys

Abys had a look that was uniquely hers, my mother said. Then she contradicted herself and said, "She had a unique look for each person." On our living room floor, I rolled onto my back, trying to understand which was true, red shag carpet threads towering over me like ancient trees.

Listening to stories about Abys hurt. Like swallowing a handful of the unsmoked cigarettes my mother'd abandoned to her ashtray, which I'd tried more than once to capture her attention. I'd stay home from school when she seemed to wake from a long trance, in one of the rare moments I could look into her eyes, to study the colors, when they were brown or green, to discover something new, undefined. Usually, cast from the TV set, a legion of soap opera characters occupied them, marched back and forth on the pupils' black screen, guarding my mother, like I always wanted to.

She claimed to have never met Abys, but the precise details in her stories made her so vivid that many women choked our living room. Many different versions stood around, cigarettes and pipes and hookahs clouding the air with smoke, all eyebrows arched in disapproval at my mother. When I attempted to put them together, to form a single person in my mind, the effort felt like an army of untrained boys trying to conquer a mountain fortress, one defended by starving mercenaries. Still, I'd inch closer and closer to her, trying to catch air from smoke.

When I was 12, in the middle of another quiet summer, I decided to search for Abys at the Zoo. My mother told me she had grown up in a small town, not unlike our small town, I'd assumed they were the same (one summer, after years of dedicated silence, I received her call and returned home to help my incapacitated father. My mother had grown eager to talk, to offer me small, literal details, as if she hoped to add tiny weights to crush down the many versions into one coherent story. Ventura beach, she said, during the Depression, near the railroad, Abys. As if the problem wasn't that I'd always believed them all and would like to forget each, however different). My matchstick legs carried me from our faux middle-class farmhouse, my shoes sparking flints against the sun-sucked black top. Our dogs and cats—we had two labs, one white, one chocolate, and two calico cats—followed me until they lost themselves in a frenzy of barking and stalking the smells of lilac and urine from boys who pissed in our town creek.

When I reached the Zoo, a seedy apartment complex known for drugs and prostitution (which I associated with the loss of family since I had spent time here with each of my brothers before they escaped home when it had been a smooth field of red dirt and perfumy, numbing manzanita) each of its windows burned with a different sun. Heat. Something had reached up and slicked my fingers, my palm. I pulled away. A sidewalk vent from the complex spat up steam. A sharp sting bit my bladder, an ambiguous, incessant throbbing, like a hand inside me stirring. I looked around for someone who might let me use their bathroom, but the buildings seemed abandoned. As I stood there feeling alone, I imagined each small apartment stuffed with boys, dozens of us herded to a kitchen to be packed in boxes, columns of boys stacked beside themselves, stored for deployment. I peeked through one of the windows to see if my intuition was right (this will sound improbable, but as a child, my mind caught glimpses of things, of undisclosed, shy places; I wished this capacity away until it atrophied and withdrew somewhere else). In the living room, five boys were doing pushups in front of a sun-glassed man who sat in a laz-e-boy chair, a man whom I intuitively thought of as the General. He wore an eclectic uniform that mixed fashion sense from different military branches. I began to sweat, or notice the sweat, on my forehead, my eyes burning, or beginning to burn, the space between my lips, a leak.

I banged on the door of the closest apartment. A woman with calico hair and a yellow crayon robe leaped out, her face blurry, like its features had been smeared with Vaseline, or clouded by a puff of smoke. Her chewing lips grew distinct first, the lipstick an unnatural color that I liked, a lilac that over the summer sometimes seemed light blue or darkish purple or white. For a moment, there was a sincere look in her eyes—the irises neon jellyfish outsmarting a murky ocean—that made me feel safe.

Abys gulped something down, grabbed my belt, and yanked me. The door's latch clicked behind us and she sat me in front of a mirror-top coffee table. Paintings of fish on the wall surrounded us—goldfish, piranha, squid—a hutch of kitschy ocean figurines—whales, penguins, sharks, waves, palm trees, lobsters and crabs and an abundance of wax parrots, parrot bookends on top of the bookshelf, parrot lovers on the fireplace mantle, a fireplace full of glittering sand. A needle gunned through my bladder, sewing together unfamiliar parts. My hands covered my barking, stalking lap. Abys ignored my discomfort, and asked if I would like some lemonade or tea or Coke or juice or water or beer. My eyelids grew sweaty at her suggestion, and I closed them, hoping to wish the images away. When I opened my eyes, she inserted a cold glass in my hand. Murky chocolate milk. It was seeping in my hand, or leaking, like there was no difference between glass and milk. A tiny puddle slicked my palm, a growing froth. I didn't want to drink anything but Abys gave me her death stare, and I noticed a new color, a hazel brown, take her eyes, and I felt sad for her, for a reason I didn't understand. The image of a porcelain toilet full of splashing milk and chocolate syrup swirls filled my mind. Feeling a little weird and a little scared, I took a drink. My throat tightened, and as I choked on it, Abys nodded, praising me and urging me to down the rest. The full feeling inside my body, not pain or pleasure, confused me, and grew. I had to let go.

The empty glass smacked the table and left a crack in the mirror. Abys ignored this, and the broken shards the accident produced. Although this didn't seem to bother her, I worried that she would freak out when she smelled the growing puddle at my feet. The double release had made me shudder, and in the mirror-top, my sweaty face—eyebrows knotted, lips sucked inside my mouth—struggled to identify itself in the ambivalent aches and spasms. I looked up to see if I'd been caught, and watched as Abys's eyes shifted color again, from hazel brown to hazel green. Her face had slicked too, and she seemed deeply pleased, I thought, perceiving my lack of control as the purest compliment.

She picked me up from the couch, slung me over her shoulder, and as my urine dribbled down her arm, she began telling me an obscene story. As we left the living room, I caught sight of the whale figurine in her hutch, which seemed to move, its lips shifting from a grin into something wider, or something smaller.

In the bathroom, Abys lowered my pants and aimed me at the toilet. Her hands seized me, squeezed like a trigger. More and more urine shot out, and she praised my pistol size. Feeling a surge of pride for a moment, then a stinging awkwardness that restored my earlier discomfort, I sought to escape the divergent feelings by shifting my sight to the bathroom window, where I found that nearby apartment again: through its window, five new boys stood in a lineup against the wall. The General, now sporting thick-lensed spectacles that reminded me of a magnifying glass, ordered them to underdress. He calculated, with a shimmering device, the length and width of each boy bicep, wrist, finger, leg, calf, thigh, etceteraetcetera. As the General announced official measurements to the group, each face suffered to remain quiet, straining to conceal its tears or triumph.

Afterward, Abys carried me to the kitchen, sat me on the counter and gazed into my eyes. I read in hers, which had gone completely green now (I asked myself repeatedly if they had ever really been any other color), total adoration. A response like this from an adult was a revelation, and despite my previous confusion, I was willing to do anything, no matter how pathetic, to sustain the attention. Abys fetched two bowls: one full of peanut butter, the other chocolate chips. She handed me a spoon and explained her technique:

Abys's Mixing Rules:

1. Dip spoon into peanut butter until fully slathered, a peanut butter spoon;

2. Remove spoon and dip into chocolate chips until fully slathered chocolate chip spoon (the peanut butter should be completely hidden now!);

3. Alternate between bites of chocolate-peanut butter and drags of cigarette.

Abys demonstrated the procedure for me. It seemed simple enough. I was excited to smoke my first cigarette. When I reached out for the spoon though, she slapped my hand and picked me up again; cradling me, she carried me back to the couch. She returned to the kitchen for the bowls and placed them on the mirror crack I'd made.

Abys sat down next to me and nodded once, indicating I should dip the spoon into the peanut butter and chocolate. I did. Abys lit her cigarette, and I waited to see if she would hand it over so I could take a puff. Instead her eyes lingered on the expanding smoke trails in the air. With the heavy spoon in my hand, I inferred those chips might fall off, so I reached out for the cigarette. Abys slapped my hand, took a long drag and then shoved her lips into mine. Smoke filled my mouth, and I started coughing.

Abys brought more dishes, placing them all around us, on the couch, the table, the floor. Chocolate milk, a meatloaf slice, orange juice, a bowl of scrambled eggs, two slices of pumpkin pie, a carne asada burrito, a vanilla shake. I didn't want anymore, but I wanted to please Abys, who left again and returned with a bowl of chili and a five-foot cheese board and arranged them in front of me like a tableau. I stared at it; Abys stared back. She gave me a thumbs up. The Merlot cheese looked good, and I thought I might get drunk if I had some, so I cut slices from the wheel, including the purple rind, and mixed them into the chili until they melted. Then Abys shredded cheddar cheese and we mixed that in and then we mashed crackers in.

Days of Our Lives was on Abys's TV. The camera shifted to do an extreme close up on the face of Dr. Marlena Evans Brady, psychiatrist heroine, a character my mother and I had spent many summer afternoons watching quietly together. Her contacts had a cheap green demonic tint. She was talking to herself for the audience, monologically extolling the merits of her grand plot to topple her once-beloved family, which she would accomplish by seducing and marrying her former archenemy, the notorious Stephano Dimera, a crime boss who controlled a vast network of mercenaries, who had recently kidnapped and brainwashed her with mind-control drugs and subliminal videos until, in this weakened state, Satan possessed her.

During the commercial break, Abys marched into the kitchen to make popcorn. I heard a can of kernels rattle into an oiled pan. They ratatatated as she shook it back and forth, then cracked open like shots from a firing squad. Before *Days* came back on, she dropped a huge drippy bowl of corn into my lap, and my overwhelmed fingers swam in butter and salt, gathering up oily handfuls. After I finished, a few hard kernels lurked below a buttery pond, and I put one into my mouth to suck the flavor. When I took the clean kernel out of my mouth, Abys told me to put it back in, at once. Hey, stupid, I made that, you're supposed to enjoy it, she said. I bit down but it was too hard and wouldn't break; instead, it ground against my teeth, rattled and dented until my jaw ached. Abys gave me her death stare, so I bit down harder until I heard it crack.

As my tooth and jaw throbbed, the room seemed to flood with smoke, and then the only thing I could hear *and* see – I know that doesn't make sense, but you can't blame me, I was in some pain – was Abys's voice. The imagery, the setting around me shifted one more time, like a camera cutting to a black movie screen, which then lit up to display an ocean and sandy shore, a beautiful scene from a beach. The camera, I guess, then panned down, mimicking the movement of someone's head plunging, and brought into focus an image of my socked feet running down a paved boardwalk. My head, or the camera, rose, and I smelled salt air and then passed a sign that said Marina Park, Ventura. The grass seemed jaggedly cut from the hot sun and the palm trees' big fronds made them feel like giant lurking flowers. My body ached, and I wanted to stop running but my legs sliced through a trail of alleys until I came out on a city street, then to Raymond Theater. My hand removed a nickel from my sock and set it on the booth's counter. I could finally breathe in the big dark room and pretended not to exist and had forgotten again to see which movie was playing. On the screen, King Kong reached out for Ann and my body felt sort of jumpy, so I wiped my hands on my dress. After the movie, I hid under my seat waiting for the next one to begin. This was the safest way to spend the night when the mercenaries came. An usher's flashlight woke me and I returned to Surfer's Knoll where I planned to sleep out on the sand, which is a good warm place to sleep even with the Santa Ana wind and I imagined walking out on the water with Ann and running really far out so that we could try scratching a hole in the moon, but then Kong's black and white hand emerged from below for us.

I was a lucky because we lived at the beach. But we lived near the railway too, so the mercenaries could find me when they stopped for rest. They travelled across the country, traveling in loud, glimmering cars for weeks and were exhausted when they stopped and my parents asked five cents for a night's rest, and before they came to my room, I escaped through a hole I'd made in the wall. Kong's hand crushed us, Ann and I, placed us in his mouth and inside the train car, the mercenaries oiled objects like guns and drank and smoked and ate food from dented cans.

Abys held the popcorn bowl out to me, urging me on. A handful of kernels floated in the butter. My jaw and stomach ached from the first kernel, and I couldn't eat anything else. Abys stared at the TV, with the bowl in her lap, silent, for the next half hour, watching the end of the show (Marlena had begun floating into the air above her bed), and I felt guilty, like I had severed our connection. I tried to think of something to do, like an idiot, and asked Abys about the plot. She gave me a brief death stare, and then I sat quietly and watched Marlena who, by the way, had stopped levitating when her husband John Black, a priest, entered. But she did it just to fool him.

The rest of the summer, Abys made all kinds of things—shrimp cocktails, spinach dip, chocolate chip cookies (these were made of chips where the dough functioned as spackling), nachos, hot dogs, lasagna, stir fry, sushi, charburgers (hamburgers with melted cheese hidden at their center), and hot fudge sundaes. It was delicious, but when I finished my sundae, my stomach began to ache, like someone had gut punched me. I ignored it and we continued on— Marlena seduced Tony Dimera, Stephano's good-hearted nephew, urged her traumatized patients on to acts of vengeance, transformed into a black panther to stalk her victims, and finally, morphed into the form of her rival, Kristen Dimera, in order to take control of John Black and Stephano's empire—with cheesecake, vegetable soup, enchiladas, turkey with dressing and giblets, and fudge peanut butter pie.

One afternoon, after a mouthful of peanut butter fudge, I bit down on something hard, something that cracked in my mouth. I spit the thing into my hand and saw a popcorn kernel. Over the previous few weeks, my stomach had an ache after meals, and then it began to ache before meals. Bloated from constipation, a distended spot had purpled my belly, had grown like an angry seed, a seed shaped like a fist. Feeling paranoid, I rubbed the spot below my shirt so that Abys couldn't see. It was an unprecedented event and I couldn't predict how she would react. As I secretly rubbed the ugly thing, Abys prompted me to finish my pie. I said no, then waited to see what she would do. Abys turned towards the TV and started woofing her pie down. She grabbed my unfinished slice without making eye contact and stuffed it down, chugged her coffee and then mine. Then she turned the TV's sound way up so that I knew she was angry.

Now when Abys brought food in – cream corn, mashed potatoes and gravy, fish sticks, rice, tartar sauce, broccoli and mayonnaise, balut – I inspected it for kernels. When I discovered not one kernel, but a bundle in each serving, I suspected that my constipation was caused by a bezoar. I stopped eating, left unfinished platefuls. Abys ignored them, the plates piling up everywhere, the stinking smells, and when plates fell and broke on the ground, she'd quietly clean it up, then bring another serving. Whenever Abys went in the kitchen, I would pull my shirt up to inspect my bezoar, to see if my fast was helping to clear it, to cleanse. No, never, the ugly purple spot remained; in fact, it grew, despite the measures I'd taken, to the size of a real fist. Of course, I was hungry, too. I would stare at those heaping plates and come close to scarfing it all down, but then the fist's ugliness, the pain it caused, reminded me to control myself, to focus. I'd have to come up with a plan soon, I knew, or I'd need to eat something and grow sick, or I'd need to starve myself and die. Eventually, Abys caught me with my finger pressing down on the fist, trying to squish it. The spatula dropped from her hand and she pulled my shirt down, then untied her apron. She tied it around my belly, explained that her "natural" treatment would make it go away.

She continued to bring food to me, too, although each time I refused. Omelets, roast beef, fried chicken, prime rib with au jus and horse radish, donuts, waffles, collared greens, kale, string beans, salads of baby lettuce, Thai eggplant with purple basil and ghost peppers, arugula, Kouign-amann, carnitas, pickled walnuts, barbacoa de cabeza. Abys's dedication to her natural treatment grew more intense. She tied a homemade quilt around me, a black tie from a tuxedo, seashells, coffee filters, a Western-style denim vest. During all of this, I began to feel dizzy and fatigued and to sleep during the day. While I dozed on and off, I could hear Abys setting plates beside me, and the smell of heavy meat, desserts, and columns of rotten food.

Sometimes I found myself sitting up on the couch awake, not knowing the time, not remembering when I shifted into that position, with my fingers unconsciously rubbing the fist. I would feel completely disgusted, rubbing the ugly thing until it felt sore. One time, as I sat there staring at myself, I noticed Abys had left one of her lighters between a couple of old plates of food, now plates of playful grubs. I grabbed the lighter and flicked it to see if it still worked. It did. I stuck my finger in the flame and liked it, this burning. I began to imagine how good it would feel to light myself up, to stay awake in this feeding. I wanted to remain conscious so I could feel myself changed by something living, a spark. In a different form, smoke or ash, I could escape what happened, escape this ugly thing. I untied the natural remedies. I intended to undress and set fire to every inch of skin, to warm up, to change each part. Seeing my reflection in the mirror though, seeing the fist reach out, as if it were in search of a target, I looked different than I imagined. I piled the remedies on the mirror and lit them up.

Running away from the Zoo, the sound of cracking glass made me fear an arrest warrant. Our dogs and cats rubbed my legs when I reached our property. A light, excited feeling came over me as I opened the door. Although everything looked the same outside, I expected something new in there.

A cigarette smoldered in my mother's ashtray. Her eyes held the TV. I sat down next to her on the red carpet and looked up, eager for a talk.

"You fat little killer," she said.

Five Fathers

My father's death was a ten year death. During that span, his room crowded with five fathers who jostled and stooged for my attention.

First Father: The Ten Year Father

The ten year father lies in bed for ten years. Bits of ten year body fall off, or need removing. Occasionally a doctor comes in, leans over to sniff my father's toes. He delivers an opinion. After he delivers an opinion, he puts his stethoscope against my chest. He shakes his head as if he can't hear anything. Great, he says. When the door slams on his way out, a toe falls off the ten year father's foot.

It looks like a small tree timbering over.

Timber.

Actually the top part of the toe puckers into a small yellow hole. I stare at the yellow. I keep staring. The tone begins to wander. It warms. It cools. It doesn't stop changing tone.

The ten year father, during this invigorating convalescence, inflates like a dictionary. The ten year father whistles like a Lifetime show. The ten year father sobs like a pen. During this span, medicine bottles climb his dresser top. I can see us in the mirror rolling down a mountain together. There we are: rolling.

We roll.

We keep rolling. There we go.

Giant medicine tablets fill the ten year father's mouth. A dam breaks; water pours in. His ten year body sharpens and urinates. To change the sheets, I place him on the ground. The sheets come off with him from the bed, stuck to sores on his back. When I peel them off, I'm holding a book.

I can see inside the ten year father. My eyes keep staring. They stare.

They keep looking.

Second Father: Home Plate Father

The home plate father is always sliding into home plate. The home plate father is the hero of the game. The home plate father wears a pinstriped uniform.

He leaps on top of the dresser, knocking medicine bottles around. He moves to the far end of the dresser where he can catch speed. His cleeted feet get a good fast start. His youthful body leaps into the air and slides into the ten year father's bed.

A Voice from Somewhere: He scores the winning run. He scores the winning run. He scores the winning run. He scores the winning run. He scores the winning run. He scores the winning run. He scores the winning run. He scores the winning run.

The home plate father lies in bed with a frown. He wants to get up and take a bow. He can't. A chalk-line bone winks from his knee.

The home plate father never plays again. (Again.)

I walk to the plate for a closer look. The chalk-line is a pencil lead. Ink.

I push the lead back in. The home plate father leaps back on the dresser top. He leaps off. He scores the winning run. He frowns. (I push the lead again.)

There again. (Again.)

Frowns.

I keep pushing.

Third Father: Uniform Father

The uniform father stares into a dark corner of the room, his face turned away from me, nude. His body is smooth and unscarred as sandpapered marble. The only marks on his body are goose bumps. The uniform father's butt, the left check, carries a tiny tremble.

A spotlight shines on his gold curl head. He turns and salutes. He marches back and forth. His balls jiggle. He stands, balls swaying, in a rigid line. An army uniform clothes his body. He starts telling "the Dachau story."

The uniform father is one of the first Allies in camp (he isn't). He sees skeletons resting in tall trees (no). He sees inky bodies in paper holes. He executes camp guards, pointing a finger at them. *Bang, bang!* A small elevator door opens in each Nazi forehead. Viscera (maybe) spatters his uniform.

This story is the uniform father's brother's story — my uncle. The uniform father's brother is the army brother. The army brother doesn't tell the Dachau story.

The uniform father spends the war on a medium-sized Merchant Marine vessel. They deliver "war supplies." The uniform father tells the Dachau story again.

He has a handsome gold curl head.

The uniform father's uniform fades away. Nude again, he begins marching and jiggling. Trembling cheeks.

Fourth Father: Dollar Father

The dollar father showers the room with dollar bills. He cradles his belly like a pregnant money sack.

Bills keep slipping from his belly sack. His eyes are sweaty coins. He begins yanking out wads of cash. He throws them up in the air. The belly sack wheezes as it empties out.

The dollars land and become season tickets. Baseball, football. There he is.

Front row over the dugout. The dollar father yells at the players on the field. He tells the manager things (he explains fundamentals).

Lying in bed, a pile of tickets land on the ten year father. All smiles. His feet fall off. The dollar father looks scared. His face crumples up like a ticket (a paper testicle).

The dollar father hurries to the bank.

He withdraws everything from my account.

Fifth Father: The Killing Father

The ten year father is always asking about death. He says that it would be good for death to come. He would like it to come now. I tell him that he looks good in this bed. We, the other fathers and I, want him to live forever. In a death bed.

This is a nice bed, I say. Look at you in this bed!

I unclench my ten year father's teeth. I push food inside. I water the ten year father. The ten year father weeps. He never blooms; he un-wilts. The ten year father cries. He weeps and cries. Cries, weeps. Weeps, cries.

It goes on like this for a while. Ten year cries.

Cries, cries, cries, cries, cries.

I think about killing the ten year father. I think about it every day.

Ten years pass. I let his tears pool in my paper coffee cup. To the brim!

Have I always been like this? I remember mocking his limp once. I threw the ball to second instead of throwing home, wanting to make the sure out. The manager father had come out onto the field to call me names. People watched us from the stands. I called him a cripple. He took a ten year walk back to the dugout.

Look at this cup of tears, I announce. These are all mine. I can drink them. Killing tears. (Brown ink.) The brown cools. It warms. Cools. (It doesn't stop.)

I stand and I stand there as the killing father puts a mask on – hey look, it's my face – and straddles my ten year father.

He rides him. *Yee, ha.*

He takes the mask off: hey look (my face).

We ride and ride him. We ride him every day. We ride for ten years.

During this span, the ten year father shrinks. Our giant hands hold the ten year father's face (tiny!). We place a kiss on ten year lips.

We give a kiss every day. We kiss and kiss. Look at us kiss!

The killing father makes pain. This death grows more each day. The pain grows and grows. The killing grows and grows. A growing killing.

Like this.

The killing father never kills. He is only killing.

I collect tears from the ten year father. The room fills with empty cups. The ten year father is dying.

The ten year father is dying.

He dies. He dies. He dies. There he goes. He dies.

He is dying.

The ten year father never stops.

A Visitor Kills Me

There's a knock at our door. There's no knock at all. No one ever knocks during summer.

The circle swells from my mouth. My jaw aches.

I repeat the memoirist's mantra: I remember, I understand, I'm a ball gag.

The visitor comes in. He doesn't come in.

My mother stuffs a circle in my mouth. It distends like summer time at the beach. Flattens like tuna. Ouch my jaw aches. Her summers were like that: an aching jaw. Her parents, when my mother was a girl, cut her body into small specks, sold them during the Depression. They lived on the beach with a train stop nearby with men on board — strangers, hobos, stowaways – who visited their two-room shack with wads of paper in their hands and pockets fell onto her and splinters on a thin wood-plank floor.

There's a ball gag in my mouth. There's no ball gag.

Whenever she tells me the story (again and again during the summer), cuts open on my arms. Words spray out. I'm nine, ten, eleven. Our summers like this.

The cigarette in her fingers always burning to ash. The smoke's always there. An orgy of circles, a thread, a knot in our rooms. When I wake, breathe us in. She's always making sandwiches. Cut into small cubes. In the summertime, she always makes them like this:

On the kitchen counter wall, an unused rotary phone. My legs splayed on a stool. The color of the 1970s cover everything. Half-smoked limbs curl in the ashtray. She lights them, leaves them to burn on the counter between us. Her fingers twist a circle, the round blade cutting a second in the lid. The lid slumps. Spray lurches out. Splintering over the edge. Drops hit the cutting board. Specks of pink twist, judder on their surface, get swallowed.

My mother cuts the sandwich into small cubes. She sets a plate and folded napkin in front of me. In my stomach, a noise, an emptying sound, a gas bubble. She aims the circle at my mouth. Pushing it past my teeth, tightening the strap at the back of my head, turning the Soap on. It's Noon, it's one, it's two. The TV echoes through our empty house: my father and brother at work. My mother shouts and makes jokes when the actors or characters kiss, the pillows around them swollen, splintering sheets. A bead aches from my mouth, a sigh, a drool. Her jokes punch the air. My eyes stare at the cubes. The actor or character on TV reminds my mother of her ex-husband. She opens her purse, removing the old polaroids. In the first picture, he's lying on his back, legs splayed. Her thumb flips through pictures, comparing him with her current husband, the size of two men, and I begin moving in the frame with them, flipping through the scene on thin sheets where I see a close up. What makes one husband good and another bad.

The air sprays and clangs as she tells the joke about my father. The room is a mixing bowl, the walls its glass. Small specks in the air, a juddering, a white froth. The ex-husband lies down in my mouth, splays his legs. My jaw aches. She finishes telling the joke. She tells it again. When I'm older, she'll share it with my nieces.

In the summertime. I repeat the memoirist's mantra.

Knocking on the front door. There's no one knocking there. A visitor knocks.

My mother gets up and lets him in. Bits of paper and wood sit on his long hair and beard, on his old, sandy clothing. He sways, side to side, lurching. I'm too young to know he was probably on something. He tells us he's there for my brother. We've never seen him before.

My mother tells him her son won't be home for hours: come inside and wait.

We stand there in the living room, listening to the soap. He removes something from his jacket. I have a knife, he says, and shows it to us. He makes a face like he's waiting for us to react, but my mother only nods and compliments it, "It's nice," and then offers to make him a sandwich. He seems surprised and nods back to her and follows her into the kitchen. I think I should call for help, but I'm afraid he'll hurt her if I don't come along, so I follow too. The knife seemed so big, I look it up later in a Sears catalogue. "A breaking knife breaks down large pieces of meat into smaller cuts. Their blades are usually around 10 inches and are curved to create leverage to break through tough skin, cartilage, and small bones."

Next to the rotary phone in the kitchen, he sits on our stool. My mother mixes a second bowl of tuna although the one she made for lunch is already in the fridge. I believe she's hiding her fear, and I'm impressed. My mother turns, spoons more mayonnaise into the bowl. Specks of pink. A white froth growing. Her summers were like this. I decide to hide my fear too. I ask him to come see something in the family room. If I lead him away, I think, my mother will be safe. She can call someone, maybe my father, on the phone.

In our family room, past old records and a drum set, past our pool table, past bird cages and her screaming parrot, an upturned litter box, and what looked like sand, I open the closet. Fish hooks, in a tangle, too many to count, hang there from our water heater. I offer them to him and he tries to pull one free. He cuts his finger, lets out a sound, a kind of cry or moan. He pushes the finger in his mouth, sucking, sucking, making sounds.

We stand there for a while, waiting for the noise to bring my mother. The visitor begins to grow sad; I can see oceans in his eyes. Afraid, I try to reassure him: she's probably called someone. The police, my father. She'll be here for us any second.

He takes his knife out and points it to the pool table. I follow him there and we get into various poses on it for my mother, expecting her to see us through the kitchen door: he places the knife to my throat and pretends to run the blade across it. He presses the tip to my eyeball, threatening to insert it into my retina. He climbs on top of me, breaths wet wood into my mouth.

A half hour of posing passes. He drags me to kitchen doorway so we can look for my mother. Across the kitchen, in the living room, we find her watching TV. He places the blade tip to my belly. He stabs me again and again, and my intestines break, everything inside splashing out.

My mother shouts at the TV and makes a joke. She takes up a cube. She puts it in her mouth.

My jaw begins to ache.

Humanseed

The cafeteria window spit glass in the air. It hovered there like a swarm of shiny bees, then swatted our plates. My tuna salad looked like it had been topped with glass seed. A brick sat on the scratched linoleum floor. D— slipped through the door, shirtless, blood staining his arms and scabby chest.

Trying to work my students up, D— picked at one of the scabs on his arm, then pealed it off like a price tag. He tucked it in his mouth. He pushed a finger in the sore, waggled it back and forth, making a red hole. Another staff came and we took hold of D—'s arms and led him out to the gazebo. We brought him down on the grass. We each held a side down, pinning his arms and legs beneath ours. Whenever I did this, a floor-assisted restraint, a FAR, I tried to do it in the grass. Concrete can cause concussions. There were staff who did that on purpose. Carry the kid to the hard spot: bang. D— began convulsing, spasming his wet arms and slicking us with blood, trying to free himself. He twisted the legs of his baggy jeans until they came down and tangled with our knees. He wacked his head into the ground until blood filled his mouth.

In our bloodsweat tug, we had to keep our faces turned away from his spit bombs, getting hit on our arms and clothes instead, for twelve-something an hour. I relished the uneventful day I'd had with my own students, Yuba House. D— was from the worst, Bunkhouse West. They were near us and I often ended up on the ground with them in hour-long tangles. We called them students, but they were clients of the state. Milhous Ranch was a Level 14, sub-acute psychiatric facility for at-risk teens. Sociopaths. Schizophrenics. Sex offenders and victims. Prisonborn. Yuba kids were the kind I liked working with: they had humanseeds. I needed something to recognize, in the few months I'd worked there, to open the door. Imagine if you could open someone up and look inside: you'd want to find human things there, not just bullets that go off in your hand. Or blood-filled eggs. J—, for example, broke a bottleneck off a *Sobe* once and tried to stick me. Later we began to talk, discuss books. Detective novels. He loved Alex Cross, so I brought *Kiss the Girls* in, with Morgan Freeman. J— had molested his younger sister, who was handicapped, and I started a band with him. When he graduated, he could play guitar. I had to find something to work with, to balance their violence, and my guilt for helping them. E— is another example. I noticed what looked like a Neal Adams' X-Men poster on his wall — the classic characters — Cyclops, Iceman, Beast, Jean Grey. I was surprised that he'd done it himself. I brought in my collection and showed him the issues with my favorite mutants — Havok, Polaris, Legion — which he drew for me, like a professional artist. E— had never thought of himself this way, or considered college. I talked him into submitting his work for a scholarship and he was accepted into an art and design college in No Cal. E— and his twin brother had burned their middle school down, and a number of students and teachers.

After D— had settled down from whatever had set him off, we released him from the restraint, returned him to Bunkhouse West. I cleaned up in the bathroom, straining in the mirror to see if the back of my head had been hit. D—'s mucus and blood had dried into hard clots in my hair. My body shivered. HIV kids. Mystery kids. Although the state sent little information, I decided to check his in-take files anyway; any information could help you infer dangers. Toxic blood and toxic subjects. The latter usually consisted of things you didn't want to speak of; family was a forbidden topic.

In the office, as I read D—'s file, I kept getting distracted by the blood on my shirt. I reminded myself to throw it away when I got home. D— was raised by his grandfather because his parents were addicts (meth). He groomed D— with porn, and after he cultivated those tastes in him, they did the same to the younger brother and sister. This went on, who knows how long, until the parents reported it. My mind kept trying to picture the living room. I imagined a red room with a dingy couch with a cheap silver VCR and a TV with vintage 1970s porn on it. I didn't really want to imagine anymore. Then the image in my mind shifted to a memory of our living room's red shag carpet with me lying next to my mother on the floor. During the summertime, and after school, we watched soaps together. Men and women, the characters, were always making love, or trying to, in fancy beds. The air smelled like smoke. My face seemed planted in a red forest. Shreds of blank paper and popcorn kernels sat next to tree trunks, like rocks or plants. I wanted to crack the hard seeds when I found them. The giant kernel's face, smooth and empty, filled the office up and stared at me. My body pushed against a door. I snapped the file shut. When I got home, I took my shirt off and stuffed it away in a dresser.

For the next month, I limited my interactions with D—. I could do this because of my promotion: Lead at Yuba House. Whenever D— was out of control — all day, all night — Bunkhouse West would radio for backup, and I'd send another staff over. I'd send another staff over because D— picked sores on his arms and legs, his face, and never healed. He kept picking one on his lower lip that made him look like a zombie. I'd send another staff over because he was "finger-banging" himself by stretching his wounds wider. I'd send another staff over because he said that the wounds were his siblings. I'd send another staff over because he would offer to blow you and grab between your legs. I'd send another staff over because he would lock himself in the bathroom and paint the walls with feces. He painted the walls and painted his body and he'd unlock the bathroom door and paint anyone he could touch. He painted himself so staff would paint themselves when they restrained him in the grass where he begged them to penetrate him. I'd send another staff over because we were only being paid 12 an hour. I'd send another staff over because I couldn't imagine a door inside him.

Not too long afterward, my supervisor asked me to move to Bunkhouse West. Our supervisors had a way of making it sound like you had all choice in the world. If you say Yes you'll be on the good list, part of the gang and possibly a supervisor someday but if not we can replace you with another body with another set of lungs. Although we liked to think of ourselves as counselors, none of us, except a handful of therapists, had degrees. Our official designation was Mental Health Care Worker, which allowed the owners to pay a low wage, and they — this is 100% true — were relatives of Richard Milhous Nixon. The Milhous family thought of us more like fast food employees than child saviors. Sure, during our three-day orientation, they went out of their way to puff us up: Richard Milhous, Nixon's cousin, always made a point of showing up for one hour each year so he could inspire us to change lives, but then he would end his speech blaming the State of California for our poor paycheck. They mandated too many staff per house (three staff for every seven students), which he called an "unnecessary safety regulation." I considered quitting.

On my first day at Bunkhouse West, I expected D— to paint me with feces. The house therapist told me that it was a rough group before I came. She was talking about the staff. They were the kind who, when no one's looking, hit and bruise kids. She hoped I was different. I felt embarrassed anyone would ever have to ask. I showed up for the afternoon shift and the therapist had seven students — younger than my Yuba kids, 13-14, not 16-18, i.e., REAL KIDS, i.e., *super* goofy — sitting around a scratched wood table, painting. Great figurists, no. Colorful and jarring, yes. Early expressionists. They painted blurry, red-faced Captain Americas with large crooked or bent shields and triangular porcupines that were supposed to be werewolves. They painted skeletons who aimed knives at pink bones or snorted orange lines and carved smiling faces into their own skulls. They painted a lot of comic book characters — they knew that I brought comics to my students at Yuba — and one boy who had PTSD painted a purple Wolverine for me, with page-length claws. Although it wasn't something advanced like my Yuba kids could do, I thanked him and did my best performance of enthusiasm. At least I found the content, if not the style, interesting. Then D—, who had heard that I liked Star Wars, painted scratchy versions of Darth Maul and Darth Vader for me. I did my best to say they were well done, thanks, but then I couldn't stop myself from saying that he should paint a Jedi, he should try to paint someone good. He said he didn't know who they were, he hadn't seen those movies, but he could paint Jedi from a movie he had seen. Later, he handed me a picture of two ponytailed men with giant, lumbering red cocks. I understood he wanted to test me. Would I hurt him or try to fuck him someday. I didn't overreact like he wanted me to. Coolly, like a Stoic or Jedi, I gave him a time out. And I also explained what was incorrect about the picture. Jedi are celibate, I said. Try again sometime, if you like. D— gave me a scorned look. I waited to see if he would blow out and go out of program, like he usually did. Then he put on a bashful smile and laughed and walked out to the gazebo, where they liked to do their time outs. After the shift, I asked the therapist if I could bring the Star Wars movies in. I assumed D— was telling the truth, that he really hadn't seen them before.

We watched the movies over the next few weeks, but D— didn't mention the Jedi painting. Bunkhouse West's behavior charts improved — less ink stains. Future kids. Future human beings. D—, of all people, had risen to our highest level, 5, which gave him special privileges, like offsite movies, camping trips, money for junk food. The therapist asked me to take a group of fives to see Redwood, which wasn't actually a redwood, but an extra-large Douglas Fir with mutated red leaves.

The hike up the trail took a couple of hours, and it was too strenuous for kids on so many meds. The sky was clear and bright blue so we had to stop every half an hour for a break from the sun. B—, one of my favorite Yuba kids, was with us, and although he could be volatile — he was schizophrenic — he was super smart about science, probably had a genius IQ, and we had fun conversations. While we sat there speculating about Redwood's leaves, what could have caused them, I noticed that D— kept itching his arms. Playing with wounds was a sign he would blow out. I felt a little panic because I was the only staff. With five kids. I thought about how dangerous it was to bring someone like

D— out here. I imagined that if he went out of control, I might have to rely on the others, who didn't like D— and wanted to keep their high levels. Trying to calm myself, I went through my relaxation techniques: breathing deeply from my gut, flexing the muscles in my body to keep loose (I've suffered crippling anxiety attacks since I was 16) and I began to realize that the scabs on D—'s arms had grown thick. This meant the itching was likely from healing and sweat from the hike (and they were on so many meds their skin often reacted to sun). We started back up the trail, but now B— was itching his arms too. I wondered if D—'s itching had somehow passed itself on to B—, like yawning. The last thing our hike needed was one of B—'s hallucinations. When odd ideas began to explode from him at Yuba, I could usually reality check him. Sometimes, though, it was better not to say anything at all: if he sensed you were worried about him, he'd pick up on your fear and his fantasy would accelerate. I'd found that putting fires out before they started usually worked best, so I asked him if something had bitten him. His eyes popped open. He started slapping his arms. It was the damn flies landing on him, he said. Laying eggs. Flies don't lay eggs inside you, I said. His eyes un-bulged and checked mine to see if he could trust me, and since he always had, B— relaxed.

At the top of the trail, things flattened out into a wide green field of ankle-length grass. I wondered where Redwood was, but then I was staring up at it. Thirty feet or so where the underbrush began, a tall Douglas Fir with red leaves. And bark. In fact, I couldn't see a single green leaf and I wondered if it was sick. It reminded me of *The Golden Spruce* by John Vaillant, which had a whole mythology built up around it. It had some cool-looking, flat rocks beneath it, and we sat down in its red-tinted shade.

We started lunch and I handed the water bottles out. I opened the cooler and everyone had ham and cheese or PBJ. D— came over and sat down next to me. He dug for something in his pocket, removed a folded paper square, and placed it on my knee. I opened it up: it was a picture of the Emperor and Luke Skywalker. Blue lightning flowed from

Palpatine's fingers, electrocuting the young Jedi. D— had a grin on his face, and it was hard to tell if he was being bashful or sly. I told D— that I liked it, but he could sense that I didn't and got up and started pealing bark off Redwood's trunk. We'd hiked so far that day without problems, I didn't want things to go bad, so I played a card that always worked. I removed dessert from the cooler. D— chose a Twinkie. He unwrapped it, then began deep-throating it. Sexually acting out lowered a student a full level, which D— knew, but when I said so, he picked up a stick and started whacking the tree's knobby old branches. The light falling through the branches darkened. B— started slapping his arms. My other students stood up, began slapping their arms too. The swarm hovered above us, seeds of glass.

The Basement

1.

His white-gloved hands grasped her hands, guiding them forward as they fed the leg to the furnace mouth. His body grew larger as the flame consumed it, the size of two or three small men at least. As his body distended, her hands broke free from his, and she sunk down on the soot-stained floor. Fanning her hands out on cement, she crept through the smoke, found the hard surface of brick, palmed her way along the wall's face. Finding a corner, she stopped to catch her breath, instead caught smoke and bitter tongue.

Through the smoke, she could see his bulk diminish, shrink, and he cried out, convulsed, came to total collapse. Steadying his body on a tumble dryer, he removed an arm and leg from its drum, fed them one by one to the furnace, then began to spasm, distend in size.

Feeling nauseated by his unstable body, she pushed backwards and felt a brick shift and crumble against her head. Turning herself around, she dug a finger between two bricks, found the gap packed only with soot. She imagined escape for the first time and began to dig.

As the brick came loose, his footsteps stalked unsteadily towards her, the hunger of white gloves in smoke. Tasting him on her lips, she kicked her legs against the floor, sprung backwards through flows of ash.

2.

She fled along narrow streets in smoke, his footsteps stalking behind, nearby now in alley brick, then closer in chimney soot.

The burnt woman waited on the corner, lit by a cell of streetlamp, scorched body starved crisp from hunger, bones stabbing skin as fire irons do, elbows and knees knotted whip ends.

She led her through a brick-jointed city of factories, curled sighs of smoke following them from piped viscera, smoldering voices gasping from curtained windows, until finally they found a stair.

Descending to bottom, they discovered a basement of women, each with a different type of burn: electrical, chemical, fire. Each stood in a trance before washers and dryers, listening to the machines spin and tumble.

Remaining at the doorway, she watched her guide enter to ask for help, but could only issue a single spark from her mouth. Nevertheless, spooked or aroused from their routine, they answered with broken violin and cello notes, an unpitched harp thrum, a Stratocaster squeal—until the laundry machines grew hot, began to dent and shudder. The shared sounds filled each body frame until they grew, expanded, became the size of two or three colossal women, newborn giantesses.

Just as the shuddering machines readied to burst, his white-gloved hands grasped her hands. He guided them forward from the doorway where she had stood keeping watch for him.

He slashed her gloved hands down, cleaving limb and bone, diminishing each woman's size and sound.

3.

She finished unloading her husband's laundry from the ticking dryer. She placed shirts and pants into separate piles on the counter. She smoothed a shirt out on the ironing board. She starched a shirt collar. She ironed a shirt collar. She starched a cuff. She ironed a cuff. While she ironed his pants, a hair came loose at her neck. She caught the hair, clipped it in place, tossed the unfolded pants into the laundry basket. She finished folding shirts, stacking them on top of the unfolded pants. Before carrying the laundry up the staircase to her husband's bedroom, she heard a sound, a sigh from the furnace. She knelt carefully down to peer into the mouth. Although lately cleaned, a small mound of ash smoldered inside. She inched forward, questioning herself, and placed her head in. The silent mouth felt calming, it made her believe she could be heard, and she spoke a single word. Enjoying the size of her booming, echoing voice, she spoke again. She spent the afternoon like this, conversing with herself, feeling a fire bloom in her head and gut, until her husband came home, began calling for her, talking and talking about the day's decisions, the day's sales, his evening plans. She pulled herself inside the furnace, watched her husband search the basement through its teeth.

Ice Cream Shoppe

Clouds fill the sky, clotting the sun with ice cream. You're in a grassy park, and your family is crawling on their hands and knees through the grass. As they come closer to you, milk spills from their mouths, and generally speaking, you're feeling really successful.

~~~

It didn't remember much. There was a pillar of ice cream. But it couldn't have a bite.

~~~

The well-dressed man, for a few moments, for a few years, forever, stood in the ice cream shoppe, staring down at the rainbow swirled ice cream that shimmered through the glass service counter.

~~~

The guy wearing a cheap suit kept staring down at it. As far as he recalled, he had never ordered rainbow flavored ice cream before. He couldn't think of a reason to stand there any longer. "Patience is a virtue," a voice in his head said. It didn't sound familiar. Though maybe he couldn't remember the sound of his own voice. Then he heard a different voice: "The meek shall inherit the Earth."

"The patient persevere," he said out loud. "The meek acquiesce." His voice didn't sound like either of the voices in his head. Patience made him imagine weak, unsuccessful men and meekness reminded him of unattractive guys who failed to marry.

~~~

The sky was clear, sunny. A hospital bed in the middle of a park. You're surrounded by strangers, one of whom, to console you, hands you a shiny red apple.

~~~

A pillar of rainbow ice cream speaks to you. You don't recognize its words but know that it's delicious and sweet. When you reach out for some, your hand passes though, catching nothing.

~~~

Ces stood there a few minutes longer. Maybe a manager would come and serve him, maybe a manager would come and ask him to leave.

~~~

He went over the details again. Three white walls, a front window, tables and chairs. Each wall had a painting of an ice cream cone: chocolate on the left, vanilla on the right, and strawberry on the wall behind the counter. The shoppe only sold rainbow though: three buckets. Did that mean something? Was it a test? He didn't even like ice cream.

~~~

He loved ice cream. The real stuff full of butter that didn't melt on your suit. He couldn't afford more than one, so he appreciated well-made products. He'd always wanted to buy one of those huge restaurant-sized buckets and enjoy it for a year, but he couldn't justify spending that much on ice cream.

~~~

If it was a test, maybe he should eat it.

~~~

Ces thought about going behind the counter. He could just serve himself up, but maybe it was a bad idea pulling such a move. If a manager came in, he'd assume Ces was homeless and call the police.

He didn't know what the word test meant, or if test was just an unpleasant sound in his head.

~~~

The well-dressed man decided to try for himself. He thought about opening the counter door until he noticed his reflection in the glass. Blue reminded him of royalty, success, commanding others to do exhausting, degrading tasks. These were worthwhile qualities that saved him from being perceived an unworthy, unlovable scrub. He never tired of looking at himself.

~~~

Ces gave it a shot. Even jail was better than waiting here. He tried the counter door but it seemed stuck. Or locked. It didn't seem to have a lock. He tried to slide it open again. He thought about knocking on it until he noticed his reflection in the glass, which made him look away. Feeling exhausted, he sat down at the small table in the corner.

~~~

The ugly failure remembered that prayer always made him feel better. His fingers wiggled in front of his face as if they were trying to remind him how. His hands. They were supposed to make a shape. An image came into his head and he decided to imitate it. First he made a fist and then he stuck his index finger out and then his thumb. A sound shot through his head. Bang!

A calm came over Ces. The letters "pynd" whooshed in his memory, like a picnic on a sunny day, then died. An uneasy feeling came over him. Bang! he remembered to say to himself. Bang, bang, bang! He didn't know what it meant, but saying that word made him feel calm, almost strong, or maybe dangerous.

Now that he was feeling better—more calm and dangerous—Ces began to wonder about the front door. Not that he wanted to leave. He did and he didn't. He wanted to leave, yes, but only after passing something. What he couldn't remember. He couldn't forget that he needed to know why he was here but the door scared him for some
~~~

reason. It seemed like a threat. He waited to feel more calm and dangerous before taking it on.

~~~

! ice cream! ice cream! ice cream! ice cream! ice cream! ice cream! ice cream! ice cream!

~~~

Maybe he had forgotten about the door (he had to be honest with himself—why had he forgotten?), but that was because he had it on the backburner. He could always return to this particular task when he was in a better mood to take it on. Rushing yourself was no good. People seemed to consider this a bad habit, or a lack of ability, but he believed in inspiration, doing things when you could do them right—and if you didn't, then they weren't right for you to do.

~~~

Bs and Rs burred in his head, then drained out.

The door. He had to remind himself to investigate it. He wanted every clue (he wasn't planning on leaving here anytime soon without an answer!) so he could leave as soon as possible.

Assuming he could leave. Maybe he was dead and this was hell, or purgatory, or hallucination, there was no way to tell. He was sure this couldn't be heaven though. That was supposed to be cool, and this definitely wasn't. Unless it was going to turn cool as soon as he figured everything out. That would be cool, which is what he expected.

~~~

Look at the homeless guy standing in front of the ice cream shoppe! Hit him with your *Peralta!*

~~~
~~~

Ces's stomach ached. He didn't remember eating since he arrived here although he didn't remember arriving here either.

~~~

Someone hands you a rotting apple. Something white is leaking out of a worm hole.

~~~

He was standing in front of a door for some reason. Through the glass was a bright milk-seeded fog. He couldn't tell how long he'd been here. He opened the door, stepped into the doorway. He couldn't see more than a few feet in front of him. If he walked far enough into the fog, he might discover what was causing the brightness. Or he might become lost in it. He didn't want to stay here a moment longer, but there had to be a reason to stay. He had to man up, power his body, assume an alpha posture. He tried to remember how. He raised his arms up over his head. He yelled.

~~~

! ice cream! ice cream! ice cream! ice cream! ice cream! ice cream! ice cream! ice cream! ice cream! ice cream! ice cream! ice cream! ice cream! ice cream! ice cream! ice cream !ice cream! ice cream! ice cream! ice cream! ice cream! ice cream! ice cream! ice cream !ice cream! ice cream! ice cream! ice cream! ice cream! ice cream! ice cream! ice cream! ice cream !ice cream! ice cream! ice cream! ice cream! ice cream! ice cream! ice cream! ice cream! ice cream !ice cream! ice cream! ice cream! ice cream! ice cream! ice cream! ice cream! ice cream! ice cream!

~~~

The small man, little boy sat down at the table in the corner and started weeping. He told himself to have a little patience and to have a little faith and he reminded himself what was waiting in the afterlife and he remembered the word pray and that praying always made him feel dangerous and well dressed and he flexed his bicep bang! bang! bang!

he prayed and began to feel sure again now and then even a little excited to know why he was here.

~~~

Something erased the word afterlife from his mind and he told himself that he'd been thinking about his past life. He could remember nothing.

~~~

A woman in a hat. He couldn't see any hair under the — cowboy hat? — no, the brim was too short. She sat next to him on the couch, watching something together. Her face had a depressed, excited look. She hated the show. He would change it if she asked. The unattractive man wondered if they ever did anything romantic together.

A tube in your mouth. Impossible to suck this stuff in. Exhale.

~~~

The well-dressed man decided that they had just finished a long day. He was the kind of man who worked a long, hard day, and then they, as they often did, stayed out late for dinner and a movie (she looked like the type of woman who enjoyed romantic comedy; he was a man of action guy or loved westerns) together. After a long, satisfying evening, she always looked this way.

Somehow she pulled off that cowboy hat.

It was an everlasting love, Ces decided, feeling strong and dangerous. He loved her long blonde hair.

~~~

A small man with a transparent tube curling from his mouth. He was lying with his eyes shut in a little bed next to a much larger machine that beeped sporadically and monotonously hummed. In fact, the whole room was a machine. The walls, ceiling, floor covered in lights.

~~~
~~~

The old man was in a hospital room. He looked like a deflated balloon. He would be dead soon. Where were his friends and family? No flowers, presents. A TV was on. He wanted to change the channel. He pointed his hand at the static -- nothing.

He was a friend or captain. The old hero might have been his patient if he, Ces, were a doctor. Bang! Dr. Ces thought. Bang! Maybe that's why his wife looked so rapturously excited. He was a fixer of men and financially mobile.

His father. Who else? The old man had a dignified look on his flaking, pasty face. Why else would Ces be in the room so long unless the guy was family?

~~~

He definitely expected something cool to happen to him. Life was so full of cool things.

The tall athletic son was able to bench press a lot for a normal-sized guy. He had a swimmer's physique. There were a lot of things Dr. Ces had wanted to do with his father but hadn't. They probably did them all together at once: the two of them in a duck blind with a golf club and fishing rod, sharing a Bud Light, praying – bang! When they were away from his mother, they always did this. He and Ces would even smoke together and share Binaca on the truck ride home.

He loved his mother Bianca. Especially her cowboy hat.

~~~

There was the one thing he couldn't seem to forget. The pillar of ice cream. It spoke.

~~~

The scared baby kicked his legs out. The table fell over. He picked his chair up and swung it in the air and then let it go. He kicked over more tables. He picked a chair up and swung it down until it cracked and
~~~

bent. His hands flexed as he swung. The strong man slammed his bent chair against the ice cream counter. The glass cracked.

~~~

It hadn't ever heard it before. Was pill a thing?

~~~

Ces stood there for years staring at the tiny glass shards. He wanted to stick a finger in the ice cream. And when he did, blood spattered it, ruining the sweet treat.

~~~

It was impossible to remove the glass shard that filled his mouth. He was told this would be cool.

~~~

It's a hundred degrees and you can't pull yourself from the store window. It's been a number of years since you had an ice cream, and today is so hot. You bend over to get a closer look, and thunk you're on the sidewalk, your head's exploded.

~~~

He picked a chair up and sat in the corner of the ice cream shoppe. After he sat in the corner his fingers began to wiggle in front of his face and then bang! bang! bang! bang! he thought *bang!* and when he was done thinking bang! he felt dangerous and calm and thought about the things he and his father must have done together and there they were in a trim, grassy backyard, so green and trim and long that it stretched as far as a park, with their gloves throwing a ball back and forth together and the smell of the grill mesquite smoke what kind of smoke? m e s q u i t e smoke next to an oval pool an oval behind a house their house a big, sturdy house inside was probably his mother and here she was dressed in a nice dress a yellow dress and fairly sexy for his mother
~~~

maybe no no this was his wife Bianca Bianca his mother had a different name an unsexy name something and she would bring a fruit salad of grapes and bananas unsexy? and together they would say a short bang! before bang! bang! apple slices before a long, rapturous Sunday and feel excited and satisfied and especially a little dangerous and calm

~~~

Dr. Ces and Bianca were in the large grassy park with his parents, on their weekly Sunday picnic. The sun was out and they were taking turns tipping each other over into the grass. When it was Ces's turn, his father, who had a clear tube running from his mouth that curled into a hole in his stomach, got down behind him on hands and knees. His mother Callista and Bianca pushed him hard in the chest, sending him sprawling over his father into the grass. The sun was out and it was time to eat. His mother Callista and Bianca his lover began crawling towards him like infants. They got along well, they had become fast friends, they shared a variety of interests, and on the day his father dies, they'll sit, like biological mother and daughter, in the waiting room, consoling one another. It would be impossible to go on without him. Without the father, without Ces. Their mouths were full of slobbery milk as they approached and crawled over him. They opened the picnic basket up and his father removed the apples and Diet Cokes. All four of them sat in a small circle together with the sun overhead as they chatted and ate the vital healthy food and enjoyed each other's company with full satisfaction.

We're the kind of family that likes sun, Ces said.

You don't always have to narrate everything, Bianca said. Comments about the sun make my back itch. They give me a rash.

We're not talking about the sun, Callista said. Don't you think he's well-dressed in powerful clothes?

Clouds filled the sky, clotting the sun with milky seed. White drops began to fall. Wind whipped the women's dresses up over their heads.
~~~

Mothers like rain, too, Ces said.

So do fathers, his father said.

I love sitting in it, said Callista. I'd do it all day because you're so beautiful, son.

I hate it, Bianca said. The rain is too damn wet and the sun is too damn hot.

~~~

The sound of slurping snapped Ces from his trance. He looked around the ice cream shoppe. All the chairs had been returned to their original position on the floor around the tables. The tables and chairs had been unbent, uncracked. The glass counter had been fixed too. From above he heard another sound: a plop. A scoop of rainbow ice cream was stuck to the ceiling, dripping and shuddering by itself. Its drops drizzled down quietly. Ces opened his mouth and caught some on his tongue. Bang! something happened. What was it? It was a special thing bang! bang! bang! he couldn't remember the name, but it was the most important thing that could happen. It was one of those moments at the end and if it doesn't come, people feel lied to and cheated.

Ces felt dangerous and calm, however, because whatever it was, it happened. He had remained strong and faithful, stayed in the ice cream shoppe, and his reward came as expected, the answer for all of it. And now?

~~~

The tables and chairs in the ice cream shoppe began to bend and crack again. The scoop of ice cream was gone.

~~~

It was definitely reasonable to expect something now. No reason to fear the future so many cool things happen to most of us most of the time.
~~~

~~~

Ask for everything everywhere! the voice said. Ask for the sun!

~~~

Swimming in an ocean of milk. The polar caps were toast. The planet was a melting ice cream scoop on a scalding sidewalk. Ready to explode. At any moment.

~~~

Ces's legs began trembling. He got down on his knees. He asked if he could leave this place. He didn't like this. He wanted to see his family.

A scoop rose in the air and hit the ceiling.

Then all of it, one by one, ascended to the ceiling, growing into a shapeless mass. It started dripping.

The trembling thing watched it drip for a long time. It could never stop looking.

Its eyes filled with thick sticky milk. It kept clearing them out so it could witness the miracle's end.
~~~

The Chalk Tree

First Memory

The waterfall speaks transparent behind me. The words fall thinly from rocks up there. I am on a big rock down here. Its rough ridges and ruts say, Lie down on our softer lids.

The surrounding pine needles pour ropey sentences on me.

Taking in their voices, my baby body, my wiggly arms and legs, calms.

I speak back. Baby babble.

We keep talking like this.

First Memory

The waterfall vomits sewage behind me, falling through the molded rocks up there. I am on slime down here, the slime rocks: their ruts and ridges cessy with mucus. This calms me.

Then the pine needles interrupt, strangling my throat with flos. The fresh smells make my baby-sized arms and legs punch and kick. They make me cry.

I stay like this until the scent of krank, something dead and ces, passes through the air. I calm down, start happily sucking pus from my thumb.

First Memory

Confetti streams like cream pies like a birthday massacre like the free market through the papier-mâché rocks up there. I am on rock sculptures down here: their rubber ridges and ruts are warm and smooth from ice cube light.

A few feet away, a dog thing, a spruce tree, terrorizes me with its banal taste. I start crying, and a gang of aluminum pine trees flash dance around me, machine gun the spruce, then serenade me like kitschy sirens. I feel better.

My doll-sized, rubber body. When the balls in my sockets rotate, I move my arms and legs. Other voices speak in my head, and from the speaker in my belly. I have to pull a string in my side to speak. I have to turn the knob up to raise my voice.

My insides are iron gears and polyethylene stuffing.

No, says M's voice. They're shredded paper and pencil lead.

M

I'm down by some tree roots hiding when I hear the sound of something moving, a scratching back and forth. I look up: Not just an arm or a leg, but M's full body, on a swing set, swinging up and down, spinning back and forth, then the other way, back and forth.

With each lift into the air, with each spin, M shifts into a giant, squat, scrawny, portly, buff, palsied, guffawing, scowling housewife, fireman, girl scout, boy scout, and never all of these at once.

M keeps on swinging, spinning, shifting. My head heavies. I have to stop looking.

I want to talk with M, but I'm not sure where to begin. I start smacking my head against a root.

M leaps off, lands lightly, heavily on the ground, leads me out of the wood.

The Tree

We stop at the edge of a large field of short grass and tall foxtail weed. Between them is a medium-sized pond and a small garden with empty rows. It's enclosed by a circle of wood and sky.

M holds a framing nail and hammer out, aims the nail at the heart of an old oak tree. With the first whack, white dust rises from the bark.

Each particle starts screaming. I look up at M, expecting M to stop.

M keeps hammering.

A Chalk Board

M hangs it on the trunk.

It's a quiet rectangle with old ghosts on it. I can't tell what the faded streaks say. I imagine a murmur, a mumble, mute marks trying to speak. I want to talk to them, I want to understand their voices.

I keep listening. I try to help them out. I keep trying to form their words.

Chalk

M holds it out.

Very sharp. A tusk of bones.

The Form

M places the chalk tip against the board, making a slight mark. It asks M to stop, sobbing a bit, but M doesn't seem to hear. Then M pauses and stares closely at it.

Hanging from a tanned skein of skin, the board has a slight tilt.

M straightens it.

M Writes

Some words. The board screams,

Krank. Brom. Asche.

My temple stings.

I catch a headache.

Our House

Where there wasn't anything before, now poof, at the edge of the field, a few feet west of tree and chalkboard, a three-story Queen Anne Victorian mansion. The roof is a gabled attic pitted and dented with black fungus. The front walls have white fish-scale shingles green from mold. The second story has triple serlian windows full of cracks or cobwebs, and the first story an oriel window that juts out a few feet, making the front room look like a cratered moon.

Behind the west side of the house is our crumgarden. Behind that our cespond, and behind that a field of strychweed, and behind that a line of sky and wood.

In front of the house, father is in a hump in a dirt pile snoring in the nude in a bright spot of sun. Skin flakes from his burnt shoulders. Hairy squiggles cover his brown rump. His ankles are hairy, dusty. His thighs pale chalk. Ants—black dots—pass in and out of his mouth.

Not too far away from father is M's swing set, which was in the wood before, but not now.

M leaps into it and starts spinning.

Our House

My blanket is layer of dirt.

While I sleep, it slips to the floor and carpets. I shovel more in bed after breakfast, a new sheet, a new blanket. Later, a new carpet.

Father's bed is on the floor. He digs and redigs his holes, and at night, he crawls around the dirt piles eagerly on all fours, then chooses a hole and buries himself.

Pinned stink bugs decorate our room. Some are pinned through the head, some through the wings or belly, some are ascra bifida, some apateticus marginiventris, zicrona americana, many anchor stink bugs, antheminia remota, proxys punctulatus, vulsirea nigrorubra, narrow mecidea, and one loxa flavicollis.

M's Room

I'm not allowed to go in. I never see M go in or out. If you try to open it, you find it locked.

The Library

M spends all night writing in it. It has books piled on top of books, and columns stacked against columns, and they look like they'll tip over and stack my head if I stand too near.

The oldest are yellow asche and a webby, pungent brom. When I go in in to ask M a question (I want the last yolkspew! I want the stinkheads!), my nose totally kranks.

Morning Prayers

After waking, we do them.

I meet M out by the chalk board. We wait for father.

After a few minutes, he shambles over with something in his mouth, drops it at M's feet. A mad, still-pecking blackbird. The broken wings and feathers are askew. The chest's voice is a banging door. They say hi. They ask for help.

I want to pick them up, bury them near the tree.

M starts the service.

Morning Prayers

Father kneels next to me in the grass in front of the blackbird. M points chalk at the word krank and I repeat it to myself like this krank krank krank krank krank krank krank krank krank krank krank krank krank krank krank krank krank krank krank until nothing else seems to exist. When I look at the blackbird now, it's changed, grown mute, its broken parts full of krank. Next M points at brom and asche and when the prayers are over, I can see krank in the grass blades, brom in the oak tree's leaves, and asche in the cesbird's eyes.

Morning Prayers

To finish, we do a sacrament.

Father rolls onto his back, disclosing the suppuration. M pokes at his underarm with chalk until the skin breaks and the head of a yellow flow pushes up.

M drinks first, then dribbles some into father's mouth.

I'm the youngest. I go last.

Our Breakfast

Father and I share the cesbird.

On my way to the garden, I twist the head off, my tongue pushing into the slack beak, flicking the cesbird's tongue and darting into the empty sockets.

Behind me, father follows along, shrieking now and then at the phlegmy feathers caught in his throat.

The Crumgarden

The rows are full of crumble seeds: the remains of squirrels, racoons, rats, cats, birds, pigs, stinkheads, deer. Growing things.

I dig up a yolkspew. The skunky seed swirls blackly in my mouth. On the way down, it bites my tongue and throat with a stinging ces.

Our Chores

It's time for them, M says.

Excited, father begins shambling around on his hands and knees. I follow him out into field until he loses me in the strychweed.

While I work, M, swings and spins in the air, pointing at things, directing me to rocks, to holes, to the roots of weed, collecting for our meals.

M lets me go on my own to see how I do. I find a silk spider sac and look closely at it. I want to see the eggs inside. I try to imagine the sound, the first words, of the spiders hatching.

M stops spinning and writes me up, a memo of understanding.

Our Chores

M asks for a progress report.

I look beneath a rock and find some grubs. M shows me how to bruise them, how to krank the skin. I follow M's directions but can't do it. My hands keep shaking. I keep imagining little sounds coming from them, tiny wails and moans. M writes me up, hands me an incident report.

Interrupting our meeting, father starts shrieking. M and I follow the sound.

We find him on his back in a ditch with a mouthful of stinkbugs.

The head of a loxa flavicollis emerges between his lips. M points at it.

The legs and wings struggle against my tongue, against the roof of my mouth. I lightly hug it between my teeth, letting it krank my throat.

Our Chores

After we're done with little things, we hunt the wood for bigger ones.

Before we go, I find my tools in the garden: a club hammer and a three-foot long sledgehammer.

Father takes off through the trees, and I quickly lose him. I find a few squirrels and racoons while I wait for him, and I practice quieting my hands. With each strike, I improve. I shatter their heads in silence.

After some time, father's howls fill the air. I see something through the trees. A bounding, fleeing doe. I hide behind a tree and track it.

As it comes closer, I set my legs and try to keep a firm grip on the handle.

The deer's lips curl, its snout sniffing my scent in the air, its mouth opening to speak. Before it can make a sound, I thump its face. The forehead caves, making a mute red hole.

I bury it in the garden. The meat will krank in three months.

Father's Bath

Father's drenched in blood. He lets it dry and clot on him but I want to clean it off.

I take hold of his clotted beard and lead him to the cespond.

He hurries along on his hands and knees, then stops to smell a dead mouse. Excited, he lifts his leg.

I yank on his beard until he shrieks and finally comes along.

The Cespond

I make him squat in it. The cespond bubbles, full of sewage and bone. The fizz comes from a small, warm mouth, murmuring somewhere inside it, hidden.

I wash his head, his chest, his legs. His body is soft, hips brown, curved, thighs pale chalk.

It takes a long time to clean anything in the cespond, but eventually the blood comes off, or gets covered by different things.

When I wash between his legs, the thing there leaks and he whimpers. I like the sound and keep washing. Mine leaks too and I undress and wash it.

I wonder what it is.

My Name

I ask M if I'm a boy or a girl.

M says a boy has a hood and ovaries. A girl has a hat and glove. The hood and hat are both inside and outside, but the hood is bigger on the outside while the hat is bigger on the inside. The glove and ovaries are also both inside and outside the body and the same size. Ergo, a boy and girl are exactly two things with nothing in common.

My Name

M says Joshua is a masculine name while Jeptha is a feminine name. Ergo, if I am Jeptha, I am a girl, and if I am Joshua, I am a boy.

Due to the law of the excluded middle, M says, you cannot simultaneously be both a boy and a girl. Ergo, you are either a girl or a boy.

I wait for the names to speak and tell me who I am. I think:

Joshua or Jeptha, Joshua or Jeptha.

The words don't speak, but the more I repeat them in my head, they somehow grow heavy and feel like something in me and then I begin to feel like both, like both Joshua and Jeptha, like both masculine and feminine, like I might have both a hat and glove and hood and ovaries.

I have to stop thinking like this because of the law of the excluded middle, and so look at M, who is a woman, then a man, then a boy, then a girl.

My Name

M says or your name could be:

Jacey Jackeline Jaclyn Jacqueline Jacquelyn Jada Jade Jaden Jadyn Jaelyn Jaida Jaiden Jaidyn Jailyn Jaime Jakayla Jaliyah Jalyn Jalynn Jamie Jamya Jana Janae Jane Janelle Janessa Janet Janice Janie Janiya Jaquelin Jaqueline Jasmin Jasmine Jasmyn Jaycee or Jabari Jace Jack Jackson Jacob Jacoby Jaden Jadon Jadyn Jaeden Jagger Jaheem Jahei Jahiem Jaiden Jaime Jair Jairo Jake Jakob Jakobe Jalen Jamal Jamar Jamari Jamel James Jameson Jamie Jamil Jamir Jamison Jan Jaquan Jaquez Jared Jaren Jarod Jaron.

The more I repeat the names, the more I start to feel like all of them.

My Name

Finally M snorts triumphantly and points his thumb, her thumb at the chalkboard, where it says, krank and brom and asche.

Jir, M says. That's it. For short, J.

I'm Mard. Call me M.

My Lessons

It's time for them. M writes new words on the board.

Flos and kath and sláin.

These are below the other words on the board, M says. If you think them, erase them. Repeat krank and brom and asche.

I practice erasing. First, I say the banned word flos until it begins to grow thick and heavy in my head, then I stop saying it. I wipe it away.

Now I repeat the word krank. Every time I say it, it grows thicker and heavier and fills more space.

The more krank grows, the more I feel something shifting, lurking behind its weight. A mumble, the voice of a ghost.

The Walk

M takes me on a walk.

As we go, M is giant woman in a smelly blue dress, M is a squat man in a grungy blue suit.

Father follows along, his nose catching scents of krank, pulling him off the trail scrambling after carcasses and ces.

M stops us and points to the branch of a cedar tree growing near our trail, points out a yellow canker. The cedar in the air makes gag. M says the beauty of flos is untruth. In truth, krank is its center.

We keep on like that all morning. M stopping, pointing out krank, brom, and asche, lecturing on the problem of flos, flos is evil, the untruth of flos, M keeps saying it so that whenever I see or smell flos —a pine cone, a bird's nest, cedar wood—my body leaks.

The Pencil

Later that night in bed, I write the word krank in my blanket. I erase it.

The pencil smells like cedar. A tickle runs over the scar on my right temple, and I run a finger over it, a trace of something.

I grow flushed when I think of M watching, opening my door, and catching me with flos. I bury the pencil under a sheet of dirt.

Then I unbury it and sniff it.

I undress. I run the pencil up and down. I place the flos in my glove or cave. I keep doing it.

The Secret

M's in the library. Father is asleep in the cespond.

My feet creep through the house, lightly grazing wood planks and carpet. My hands nudge rooms open, the desks and drawers and margins I check for dull and sharpened pencils, broken pencils, pencil shavings. I collect all these and spread them out on my pillow, sheets, blankets, and mattress. I undress and smear myself with shavings. I place one, two, three pencils inside me. I place four, five, six. Seven, eight, nine. My glove or my cave like it.

After that, I scout the house for more. I search behind every piece of furniture. I investigate every corner.

I steal all the pencils.

The Discovery

It happens the next morning. I'm late for morning prayers, exhausted in bed, still having not slept, covered in pencil, when M opens the door.

My Punishment

M leaves my room and then returns with the book *Three Essays on the Theory of Krank*, tears the first page out, then staples it to my face.

I can't see now, so M cuts holes for me, slashing chalk through the page.

Ink seems to run from the paper, onto my skin, into my eyes, my face a mask.

My Sickness

In the dark, my eyelids stuck, grasping to see, a roughness, some damage, scratching against my stinging eye. In the dark, my body crumbles and seeds the dirt, makes strange baby sounds, babbling a flow of drool from my chin that drips a small mud puddle on my chest.

I begin to imagine things.

First Memory

I babble with the water, rock, and pine until the waterfall up there thins and loses its voice. Everything quiets. Down below my rock, muckmoles push up from the exposed sand, speaking chitter. Their swollen eyes pulse with the rhythm of their throbbing, ballooning heads. They ask the air to spread.

The dog steps out from somewhere unseen, gently straddling me with its paws. It's horse-sized and hairless, skinned in places, swathes of it gone. Its wet, thick, wrinkled, veiny, pink and grey, very saggy, clayish. A sheen of blood covers its face. Clots and scabs ring its eyes, its mouth.

First Memory

The dog scares me at first. But then something in its face, its lashless eyelids, its re-wetting lips, tells me to touch it, to hear its scars and sores. When I do this, its eyes widen, its iris colors, a light blue squid swimming in an ocean of black ink. My hand rests on the muzzle, reading the pattern, and we breathe together, an exchange of what still waits to be shared. When it draws air in or out, I do too, and then we pause and linger on a breath, on something withdrawn, something yet to be said.

First Memory

The dog's tongue unfurls, flicking back and forth inches above my body. It keeps doing this until mine rises from my mouth and joins in, without touching, licking air particles, creating an iris fizz, some strange new object made from the hidden of us.

A bubblefoam begins to flow from the fizz onto the muckmoles, who tunnel back down through the sand to their eggs.

First Memory

The dog's mouth starts bleeding.

Its eyes close. The dog leaves. It returns to its place. Somewhere else.

On the rock lid next to me, a white powder. I try to escape it, whatever it is. I start crawling away.

I'm slow. It takes a long time to cover a few feet.

It takes me a month to enter the wood.

My Schedule

Time passes. I don't know how long. Months or years. I recover from my sickness. I stop imagining things, false memories, M calls them, and return to work.

On my first day back, M hands me a piece of paper. It has a chart on it, a table:

8: J is at morning prayers.

9: J is at breakfast.

10-12: J is doing morning chores: Father's bath, finding seed for the crumgarden, watering the cespond.

1: J is at lunch.

2: J is at afternoon prayers.

3-6: J is doing afternoon chores: Finding seed for the crumgarden, watering the cespond, preparing dinner.

7: J is at dinner.

8: Dinner clean up.

9: Music time (learn songs from *Let It Krank* and *Flos Will Tear Us Apart*).

10: Bedtime prayers.

11-7:59: J is in bed. J stays in bed. J is asleep.

My Safety Manual

Along with my schedule, M also hands me this. It provides detail on how to perform my daily tasks safely. It's called *Safe Krank. A Step-by-Step Instruction Manual on Living a Life Free of Flos.*

I open it up to page one. It says, "If desires for flos persist, the following steps are required:

1. Repeat centering mantram ("krank" ad infinitum).

2. Gather rope, nails, and framing hammer (nails should be at least 8" in length).

3. Coax father from weeds (most likely location).

4. Place father between tree roots. Aim framing hammer at forehead and strike once.

5. Place father's hands together over head, aim nail at palms, then strike until hands are secure.

6. With nail, prod father's suppuration. Quaff until norming takes. Norming time varies on flos intensity. Norming manifests as desire for chore.

The Dog

One morning after I wake up, I have to pee. I go out to water the cespond when a dog comes out of the woods. It has shaggy brown and white hair with water blue eyes and floppy black ears and a wagging tail.

M's in the house writing. I don't have my manual with me. I'm not sure if the dog is flos or krank.

The dog lowers its head. It smells like ces. It's at least partially kranked. But what follows from partial krank?

Its muzzle rubs against my knuckles. The muzzle is smooth and wet. The dog begins licking my hand and I touch its head with the other. The fur is soft and warm. The dog is flos too, and I'm unsure what to do.

There's something else too, a third thing, something not krank or flos about the dog. Something old. Something I don't think is real.

I imagine the dog's talking to me. I want to respond, but I'm not sure what to say. I feel like my tongue knew once, that it had words for this.

I do my best to speak back. I play with its floppy ears. I pat its head.

Father and Dog

Father shambles over on his hands and knees next to the dog. Then he stands up and pats the dog's head too.

The dog turns from me and begins licking father's hand.

The Beginning

Father starts sobbing, ties his beard into knots. He calms down and speaks. He tells the origin story.

"The Genesis of Krank," he intones. His voice sounds really serious and deep. I imagine a pine needle that takes a few weeks to move, to start a quiver.

A ladybug emerges from father's knotted beard. It skitters across his shaggy cheek, leaps on top of his head.

The Chase

M slashes the dog's muzzle with chalk. It runs back to the wood. Father falls to his hands and knees, starts howling.

He follows after the dog. M follows too, after father or the dog.

Before M leaves, M tells me to stay. Or else.

Waiting for Dog

I go to the crumgarden and look for things the dog may like. I place a bowl of mashed yolkspew, stinkheads, and kranked deer near the edge of the wood.

Lunch time passes. No one returns. The manual says that in case of the unexpected, follow the daily schedule. What comes next on the schedule is afternoon prayers.

I go sit in front of the chalk board. I stare at the word krank and I repeat krank krank krank krank and then I find myself thinking of the dog's smell and the dog's hair and the dog's muzzle and then I think of the cedar and the flos and my glove or cave tells me it's time to find where the pencil is hidden.

M's Room

I search our house. I search all the rooms. I search its corners, behind things, underneath all objects, with no luck.

I decide to go to the library, which, with M absent, I'm not allowed to enter. The door is always ajar.

I peak in. Columns of books. My feet sneak silently through the room, careful not to knock anything over, because one thing knocked down will lead to many knocked down.

There are titles I haven't seen yet. *The Brother's Krank. Flos House. Against the Asche. Flowers of Brom.*

I find machines and tools M uses to make books, a closetful of paper.

The only room I haven't searched is M's room.

M's Room

To search it, I need a key I've never seen before. I've never seen M go in or out.

Not knowing what else to do, I look up "M's Room" in my manual.

It says, "Never break in here."

M's Room

I return from the garden with the sledgehammer.

Before I break the door in, I take a step back, try to think of an excuse, a lie, something I can say to M. Instead, my body carries me forward slowly, something unseen, a whisper calling.

I make a hole and peak in, expecting nothing, an empty room. Instead, there's another library, this one much bigger and full of bookshelves, no stacks.

I break in, find nothing but books.

Their titles are like M's books. None are written by M.

Missing

I go outside and wait. I sleep outside near the pond and listen to it bubble. I'm waiting for a sign of the dog. I keep seeing its face.

In the morning, I go over to the chalkboard for morning prayers. I sit down and wait for M and father.

After a while, I open my manual to see what to do. The word krank stares back at me, silent. Below it, the word flos. When I look away from it, it makes a sound.

I get up and start walking towards the wood. Before I go in, I look back at our house. Its form is wavering in the air, there and not there, and I wonder if it's a trick of the light. Poof, it's gone.

The crumgarden and the cespond have changed too, back to an empty garden, a pond.

The only things that remain are M's swingset, M's chalkboard.

The Search

In the wood, I lose interest in father and M. I stop searching for them. The ruts and grooves in the trail, the flos in the air, tell me where to go. I keep going until I find a tree, a red cedar. I rub the greyish red bark, rub my mask against it. I rub the extended branches, the fan-shaped, scaly leaves.

First I break a few twigs off. I put them inside. Then I break larger branches off. I stuff myself.

I strip everything from the tree. I strip the bark.

Eraser

I rest between two large roots. I close my eyes, trying to imagine the dog again. Only the word flos appears in my head. I look up at the tree limbs swaying in the air. I cut the tree's skin. I try to dig in. The wood is thick and silent. My fingernails start to break. I bite the tree and my teeth chip. I pound my fists, pound my head until I hear something moving, a scratching back and forth.

M's there, swinging, lifting high into the air, leaping at me.

A tusk of bones slams into my head. A chalk tree. An eraser.

www.ingramcontent.com/pod-product-compliance
Lightning Source LLC
Chambersburg PA
CBHW022159160726
48282CB00024B/255
* 9 7 8 8 1 1 9 6 5 4 3 8 3 *